401 WAYS
TO SUCCEED
AT ONLINE DATING
with psychology

JAY P. GRANAT, Ph.D., LMFT

ISBN: 979-8-35090-867-1

Millions of people around the world search for love through online dating. What does it take to be successful? Why do some people fail at internet dating? This book contains dozens of psychological strategies to help you or someone you love succeed in the search for love. While online dating can be challenging and stress, it is rather amazing that single peope now have instant access to millions of other single people.

MY EXPERIENCE WITH ONLINE DATING

My lovely wife of thirty-two years died approximately three years ago.

We were very happily married. We were a terrific team. We had a lot of fun. We knew how to listen, how to be kind, how to be flexible, how to parent, how to be open-minded and how to treat each other with kindness, dignity, and respect.

My years with Robin also provided me with a framework for understanding what it takes to have a healthy relationship and a thriving marriage.

Unfortunately, my wife developed a malignant brain tumor which ultimately took her life. She was a heroic warrior who rarely complained and she played a key role in helping to improve the right to die laws in New Jersey. We also raised quite a bit of money for two important charities. We managed to "turn lemons into lemonade." I felt this was important for my kids to see this and to be a part of this fundraising process.

During the course of Robin's illness, we discussed openly and candidly what I would do with regard to finding a new companion. Robin said I was a terrific man and a great caretaker and she did not want me to be alone. She encouraged me to find someone very special.

So, two months after Robin passed, I decided to start dating.

Robin and I met the old-fashioned way - at a party. I did know a fair amount about online dating because I had counseled many patients who were using these sites and various apps to find a new companion. Some of these people were young adults who had never been married. Others were divorcees, separated or widows or widowers.

I helped many of them to remain calm, confident and focused as they embarked upon what can be a very challenging journey. I assisted them with their profiles and helped them to identify the kind of person they did not need and recognize the kind of person who would make their life richer.

I have dated approximately ninety women during the three years since my wife has died. I will tell you more about my adventures and experiences later in this book.

This book will include advice, tips, guidance and suggestions based on my personal experience with online dating and my clinical experience counseling, guiding and providing psychotherapy to clients in my practice. As you will see, there is some repetition in this document. This is intentional as there are some tips and concepts that are really essential.

I will also show readers how they can use sport psychology techniques, hypnosis and what I call cognitive behavioral dream therapy to manage, navigate and succeed at online dating.

When I started writing this piece, I thought I would generate perhaps two dozen tips. However, I kept working on it and as of this writing there are more than for hundred tips and ideas in this book.

A LITTLE MORE ABOUT ME

I have been a psychotherapist and a licensed marriage and family therapist for about thirty-six years.

During the course of my career, I have counseled thousands of people. Approximately half of my practice was devoted to relationship counseling.

The other half of my practice involved my sport psychology work with elite athletes, young athletes and weekend warriors. Interestingly, some of the mental toughness training that I did with athletes proved to be useful for the single people who were searching for companions online.

With regard to my relationship counseling, I helped people solve marital problems, relationship problems, separations, parenting issues and divorces.

In brief, because of demand, I became a therapist/coach with some expertise in guiding people through the healing process and then coaching them through the dating, meeting and mating process.

Given my clinical experience and my personal experience with online dating, I think I have a deep understanding of what people need to do to avoid failure and be successful as they utilize digital technology to find Mr. Right or Ms. Right.

Obviously, not all of these tips will be relevant for you. If you get a handful of ideas that resonate with you and that you implement and find useful, this book will probably be enjoyable and helpful.

Let's begin with two important questions:

Are You Really Ready To Start Dating?
When Is The Right Time To Start Dating?

Having counseled and coached hundreds of patients about dating and relationships, it is apparent that people recover from the loss or from the end of a relationship at different paces. Some people need time to heal and do not want to date until they feel ready. For example, I have had patients who waited two years to start dating. Others want to "get back in the game" more quickly because they are eager to find another lover/companion.

Online dating can be an exciting adventure for some individuals. Others find it quite uncomfortable and feel embarrassed about the idea of searching for a lover in this manner.

For me, my wife was ill for almost two years and I felt I was ready to socialize with women and curious about who I might meet a few months after she passed.

As I said earlier, I had a terrific partner and a marvelous marriage. I like being connected to someone and I feel like I have a very good understanding of what it takes to build a solid relationship.

Moreover, I think of myself as a resilient warrior who refuses to give up when life throws me a curve or knocks me down. Knock me down ten times and I will find a way to get up the eleventh time.

In addition, I know myself well enough to know that I like being connected to a partner. So, I might as well do what I can to discover this connection.

Last, no one who I know is getting any younger. So, to me, it makes sense to "get back in the game."

LET'S DISCUSS A FEW DO'S AND A FEW DON'TS

1. Don't lie about your age.

2. Don't lie about your height.

3. Don't lie about your weight.

4. Don't lie about your interests.

5. Don't lie about your marital status.

6. Don't post pictures that are from a previous decade.

7. Have professional photos taken.

8. Include full body shots.

9. Include several head shots.

10. Consider a few photos of you engaged in some of your hobbies. This will help potential respondents to get a sense of what you are passionate about.

11. Appearance is important in this search. Everyone wants to be with someone they find attractive.

So, get on a healthy eating regime and an effective exercise regime.

SAFETY ISSUES

1. There are some troubled and dangerous people out there. So, meet in a public place.

2. It is easy to do background checks by using tools on the web. In addition, you may want to do a Google search on a person before you meet. I suggest you use these tools to stay safe.

3. Be protective of your address, phone number, financial information and email.

4. Don't invite a new date into your home until you know them.

5. If you become aware of the fact that a person is lying to you, run the other way.

6. Linda Jenkins, in her book, has identified the ten things people lie about online: Age, Height, Single Status, Addictions, Cars/ Transportation, Job-Employment, Relationships-Marriages, Family, Money and STD's.

7. Be on the lookout for people who drink too much, use illegal drugs, smoke pot daily and self-medicate.

8. There are a lot of con games online. So be careful with your personal data and information. Obviously, stay away from a person with a criminal record.

9. If you date or meet someone who shows signs of being violent-remove yourself from this relationship immediately.

10. If you encounter someone who stalks you, consider getting a restraining order.

YOUR BIO /PROFILE

1. Your bio or profile is very important. Like it or not, you are competing with other people who are looking for Mr. or Ms. Right.

2. Your profile is like an advertisement for yourself.

3. if you are looking for a hookup, you need a different kind of profile than you need if you are searching for a long-term relationship. The "hook up" profile should be brief, fun, inviting and flirtatious. It should also include some attractive full length photographs.

4.   I have written many "hook up" profiles and "relationship pro-files" for my clients and I believe that there is a lot of psychology involved in generating an effective profile.

5.   Years ago, I taught college courses and graduate school courses on the psychology of advertising. I also wrote a book on adver-tising psychology and I was hired as a copywriter for businesses that wanted copy that was based in psychology.

So, I think I know what I am talking about where your profile devel-opment is concerned. Your bio needs to follow the old advertising formula known as AIDA. Attention, Interest, Desire, Action.

You need to tell a lot about yourself and about the kind of person you are seeking. But, you need to do this in an appealing manner. I think a bio should be between two hundred and fifty words and five hundred words. If you hate writing, consider hiring someone to help you with this document.

Feel free to reach out to me, if you would like me to assist you in this process. You can email me at info@stayinthezone.com or call me at 888-580-ZONE.

HOW TO CHOOSE THE RIGHT DATING SITE

1.   There are a multitude of different sites from which to choose. Some are long-term relationship oriented. Others are focused on casual sex and hook ups. Know what you are looking for and choose a site or sites that align with your goal. This book focuses primarily on people using online dating to find a LTR (Long Term Relationship)

2.   Don't limit yourself to just one site.

3.   Don't give up on the old-fashioned ways of meeting.

4.   Networking and introductions can still be useful.

5.   Try using MeetUp.com to meet people who share interests with
     you.

6.   Experiment with different sites.

7.   Consider using a matchmaker or a reliable dating service.
     However, be very careful when using a dating service as I have
     had a number of patients who spent large sums of money and
     felt that they were "ripped off" by some of these organizations.
     So, do your research carefully before you turn your love life over
     to a dating service or a matchmaker.

WHAT KINDS OF QUESTIONS SHOULD YOU ASK ON YOUR FIRST DATE

Some people get quite anxious prior to meeting a new date. If you get anxious before a face to face meeting with a new person, here are a few questions that may help to stimulate conversation and help you to become relaxed and self-confident while you learn about the person who is sitting across from you.

Notice that a lot of these questions are about interpersonal relationships. Realize that you can learn a lot about a person by learning about their friendships, their family and their colleagues.

1.   Where do you live?

2.   Where did you grow up?

3.   What were your early years like?

4.   What kind of work do you do?

5.   So, what is a typical day like at your job?

6. How did you get into that field?

7. What are your hobbies and what do you do for fun?

8. What is on your bucket list?

9. Where did you go and what did you do on your very best vacation?

10. Tell me about your relationships with your kids and your family. If the person is divorced, separated or widowed, you may not want to ask too much about their former partner on a first date.

11. Do you have any childhood friends or friends from a long time ago?

12. What has your online dating experience been like?

13. What was the funniest date you had?

14. What was your worst date?

15. What was your best date?

16. What kinds of music do you love?

17. Where did you go to school? Why did you choose that school?

18. When are you most peaceful?

19. Would you like to get together again? Perhaps we can play tennis, go bowling, check out a museum, go to the park or take in a ball game?

A FEW TIPS ON COMMUNICATING EFFECTIVELY

1. Periodically paraphrase what your date is saying so that he or she knows and feels you are interested and engaged.

2. The more you share about yourself the more he or she is likely to share about themselves. Psychologists know that there is a lot of research to support this concept.

3. If you are recently divorced or separated and if you are somewhat wounded and bitter, you may want to avoid conversations about your ex.

4. Do not try to get to know everything about a person on a first date.

5. As I say elsewhere in this book, the main objective of date number one is to determine if you want to have a date number two with this individual.

6. Lower whatever anxiety you might have and remind yourself that you are simply having a chat with another human being.

HOW TO IDENTIFY A GOOD MATCH

1. If you are a white collar professional, you probably need a white collar mate.

2. If you are well educated, you need someone who is a peer.

3. If you have kids at home, you need someone who is okay with your children.

4. Do you need someone who is the same religion as you?

5. What is the best age range for you?

6. You probably need someone who shares some of the same interests that you have.

7. Dating a widower or a widow is different than dating someone who has been divorced.

8. Avoid dating someone who is separated or still living with their spouse.

9. Look for someone who "leans in" to you when you are discussing something important.

10. Since a lot of couples break up over money issues, look for someone who is a financial peer.

11. Look for someone who has complimentary skills and talents.

12. Traveling can present some challenges for a relationship. So, find a partner who you can travel effectively with.

13. Try connecting with someone who can teach you things you do not know about.

14. Find someone who you like to do nothing with. That is, just being together is fun.

15. Learn from previous mistakes you have made in relationships. Do not make the same mistake or wrong choice over and over again.

16. Spend some time visualizing in great detail who is a good match for you.

17. Look for someone who is a good teammate.

18. Find someone who you enjoy doing things with but who also gives you space and autonomy.

19. Find someone who makes you feel very special.

20. Find someone who treats you with kindness, dignity and respect.

21. Do not waste time and/or energy if you encounter someone who says they will get back to you and they do not follow through with this plan.

22. Be ready to spend an hour a day on this search.

23. Prepare yourself for some complications and disappointments. People are complicated and relationships can be exponentially more complicated.

24. Pay close attention to how the two of you problem solve as a team. If you can solve big problems and small problems easily, you may be a good match for one another.

25. If each date with a particular person gets better and better, you may be with someone who is very special.

26. Remember, it can take six months or longer to really get to know somebody well. I recently dated someone and all was going well until she did not get what she wanted and she had what might be thought of as an adult temper tantrum. She got quite upset over a very small issue. I ended this relationship shortly after I saw this side of her. The last thing I need at this point in my life is someone who is rigid, demanding, emotionally immature and unwilling to compromise.

27. Sometimes, I encourage clients of mine to get to know someone during The Winter, The Spring, The Summer and The Fall.

28. If you feel really lucky to have your mate in your life, you are probably on the right track.

USEFUL QUESTIONS TO ASK YOUR DATE DURING YOUR COURTSHIP

Here are some useful questions that can help you to get to know your love interest.

Some of these may not be appropriate for a first date, but they can be useful in getting to know each other when and if a relationship starts to evolve.

These questions can help to determine your compatibility and they can also identify some warning signs which may create conflicts and stress as you move forward.

These questions are intended to stimulate conversation, help you get to know each other, identify possible warning signs and assess the synergy between the two of you.

Some of these questions can be quite challenging. Some of them can be fun to explore together.

Some people find it useful to contemplate the issues raised in these questions on their own.

Some individuals may want to explore these issues in the presence of a therapist.

Warning-Do not ask all of these questions at one time. Your partner will feel like he or she is being interrogated.

And do not ask these kinds of questions early on in the relationship. They can be intimidating for some people and you don't want to turn people off.

1. When are you most peaceful?

2. What is the toughest thing you have had to deal with in your life?

3. What are your earliest happy memories or sad memories?

4. What was your childhood like?

5. What were your family vacations like?

6. What were your family dinners like?

7. What kinds of things are on your bucket list?

8. Tell me about your best friend or best friends?

9. What was your last relationship like?

10. What would you like to know about me?

11. Tell me about a typical day on your job?

12. What is your relationship with your kids like?

13. How did you choose your career?

14. What are your dreams for your future?

15. What was the most joyful thing you have ever done?

16. What is your earliest memory?

17. What caused your marriage to end?

18. What was your parents' marriage like?

19. What is your relationship like with your siblings?

20. What do you do to solve interpersonal conflicts?

21. Who are the most important and influential people in your life?

22. What is the dumbest thing you have done in your life?

23. Describe relationship builders?

24. Describe relationship damagers?

25. Can you think of a couple that has a super relationship? Who are they?

26. Tell me about your best friends?

27. What are you really bad at?

28. What are you really good at?

29. How do you manage your money and finances as a team?

30. Are we good partners where sex, intimacy and affection are concerned? If not, what can we do to improve in these areas?

31. What can get you really frustrated?

32. How do you know you are in love?

33. How do you know if it's a healthy love?

34. What is your experience with religion like?

35. What would you like your life to look like in five or ten years?

36. What do you like to do on a Sunday morning?

37. What makes for a joyful sexual life?

38. What are your feelings about alcohol use?

39. What are your feelings about marijuana use?

40. What are your feelings about tobacco use?

41. What are your thoughts about a couple managing money?

42. What are your thoughts on having children or living with children?

43. What were your previous relationships like?

44. What was your best relationship like?

45. What was your worst relationship like?

46. What are your feelings about pets?

47. What is the funniest thing you have ever experienced?

48. Tell me about your best vacation or travel experience?

49. How do you manage stress, anxiety, frustration, sadness and depression?

50. What sports do you like to play?

51. What sports do you like to watch?

52. What was the best job you have ever had?

53. What was the worst job you have ever had?

54. Have you ever been in therapy? If yes, what did you work on and what did you learn?

55. How can you recognize a dysfunctional relationship?

56. How can you determine if you are good teammates?

57. Do we treat each other with kindness, dignity and respect even when we are arguing?

58. Do we make each other's lives easier?

59. Do we have a lot of fun together?

60. Do we focus on each other's good qualities?

61. Do we know what we are good at and bad at?

62. Who do you look to for advice and support in your life?

63. When is it time to end a relationship?

64. What was your parents' relationship like?

65. Tell me about your heroes, mentors or role models?

66. Describe your worst love relationship?

67. Describe your best romantic relationship?

68. How did you choose the college you selected?

69. Who is your oldest friend?

70. What is your favorite movie?

71. Who is your favorite author?

72. What is your favorite book?

73. Describe your typical day at the office?

74. What is the dumbest thing you have ever done in your life.

75. What do you when you are home alone?

76. What do you like to do with your lover?

77. What are your weaknesses?

78. What are your strengths?

79. When you spend time in a person's home take note of photos, momentos, orderliness and the overall ambiance. You can learn a lot about a person from these observations.

80. What do the two of you do really well together?

81. What is really terrific about our relationship?

82. Do you believe in spirituality?

83. Do you believe in an afterlife?

84. What are your goals in your life at this point in time?

85. What is the one thing you need to do to improve, grow or strengthen your current relationship?

86. How would you rate our relationship on a scale of 1-10. One equals a terrible relationship and ten equals an outstanding relationship.

87. What is one thing we can do to improve our relationship?

A FEW ADDITIONAL TIPS ON GETTING TO KNOW SOMEONE

In addition to talking to the person you are dating, there are a few other things you can do to get to know someone.

1. When you visit the person's home, apartment or dwelling, pay attention to his or her hobbies, the condition of the residence, photos of family members, photos of friends, art work, music library, the location, etc.

2. As noted earlier, a person's family and friends can tell you a great deal about someone's character and personality.

WHEN IS THE RIGHT TIME TO HAVE SEX WITH ONE ANOTHER?

I could probably write an entire book on this question. But, I will be brief here.

Some of you who are reading this, may want to be intimate with someone on a first date.

According to one woman I dated, she believed that date number three was the correct time to get sexually connected with a person. Apparently, some people have supported the idea of being intimate on date number three. I do not believe that there is one right number for everyone.

Do what you are both comfortable with and have some adult discussions about this to get a sense of where the two of you are and what is right for both of you.

Pay close attention to flirtatious cues, body language, physical contact, the way people dress and the way you look at one another. Sometimes, people discover the right time and place to be intimate quite naturally. One woman who I dated simply invited me to share her bed with her rather than me drive home late at night. This gesture began a nice sexual connection. Unfortunately, the relationship only lasted a few months.

Some people like to approach sex in steps, beginning with making out and foreplay. Others like to move directly into being quite intimate with each other.

This brings another important thought related to sex. Now, great sex is wonderful. However, sex is just one component of a love relationship. Some people think and behave as if it is the most important part of a love relationship and they overlook other core building blocks of a long-term relationship.

HEALTHY RELATIONSHIPS VS. UNHEALTHY RELATIONSHIPS

Because I have done a lot of marriage counseling and relationship counseling, I have seen people who, unfortunately, spend too much time suffering in a toxic, dysfunctional marriage or relationship.

To learn more about healthy relationships, spend time observing couples who appear to be great teams. Notice how they communicate and how they problem solve.

Also, remember this simple concept:

"A healthy relationship is easy most of the time and occasionally challenging. A sick relationship is challenging most of the time and occasionally peaceful."

AVOID NARCISSISTS AND BORDERLINES

1. Having a healthy, loving, and supportive relationship is virtually impossible if you are involved with someone who has one of these two diagnoses. These personality types tend to be very difficult to treat.

2. There is a treasure trove of information online about these disorders. Educate yourself a bit so you can avoid the stress of being romantically involved with a narcissist or someone with a borderline personality disorder.

DRUG ADDICTS, SEX ADDICTS AND ALCOHOLICS

Similarly, a drug addict, sex addict or alcoholic is a very bad choice if you are searching for a lifelong companion. Workaholics can also be very challenging. And some workaholics are narcissists.

AVOID PEOPLE WHO HAVE BEEN VICTIMS OF ABUSE

People who were subjected to emotional abuse, physical abuse, sexual abuse, incest, rape, violence or traumas can often be difficult to be in a love relationship with. This is particularly true if the abuse happened early on in their lives. People with these kinds of histories frequently need and can benefit from intensive psychotherapy.

PEOPLE WITHOUT FRIENDS

People with few or no friends can be a sign of some trouble or difficulty where relationships are concerned. You don't need to have a lot of friends, but people without a support network probably do not offer very much to other human beings.

Conversely, someone with a group of good friends probably knows how to be a friend someone else.

DON'T CONFUSE INTELLIGENCE WITH A HIGH EMOTIONAL IQ

I have dated a number of very interesting and intelligent people. These have included doctors, lawyers, CEO's, Ph.D.'s and successful entrepreneurs.

However, as I discovered, some of these "very bright people" had very little emotional intelligence. They were lacking in communication skills, self-awareness, problem solving skills and relationship building skills.

For me, this was a reminder that intelligence and emotional intelligence are different characteristics.

To be candid, of the sixty-seven women I dated, three of the attorneys and three of the physicians were very troubled people and quite dysfunctional. Perhaps it is because they spend so much time developing their careers that they neglect the development of their emotional intelligence and their interpersonal skills.

Please understand that I am not intending to criticize females who are in demanding professions. Rather, I am simply reporting some of my own experiences. In fact, I am drawn to females with interesting and challenging careers.

MORE TIPS ON DATING IN A RATIONAL AND EFFECTIVE WAY

1. Consider some phone calls, some texts, Facetime or Zoom meetings before you meet in person. I think three contacts before you meet is a good idea.

2. Accept the likelihood that you will have more bad first dates than good first dates.

3. Remember, just one outstanding person can change your life for a lifetime. So, hang in there.

4. Gear up for an emotional marathon and expect to stumble, expect to fall and accept the fact that you may be injured during this journey/adventure.

5. Consider location and don't date someone who lives a distance that is too far to visit three times a week, just in case a relationship develops.

6. Be an astute listener on your first date. Read Dale Carnegie's book How to Win Friends and Influence People.

7. Avoid lengthy conversations about your ex.

8. Ask open ended questions to keep the conversation going.

9. If you are a recently divorced person and still somewhat bitter, avoid conversations about your attorney or your spouse's attorney.

10. You don't have to reveal your entire life history on date number one or on date number two.

11. Avoid conversation about painful and negative subject matter until you have formed a relationship. Keep date one light, fun, friendly and easy.

12. On a recent date, we played pickle ball and then we went bowling on a first date. It was terrific. I called it "Camp Day."

13. Avoid taking advice from people who are not involved in and experienced in the online dating universe.

14. If you have friends who are using internet dating, share your war stories, your funny stories, your advice, your experiences and your love and support. I have two friends who are actively using online dating. One is an intensive care doctor and the other is a Ph.D. It is really helpful to touch base with them from time to time. I am an independent thinker, but they understand this world, provide support and love and can offer some useful advice and helpful insight into this method of meeting people.

15. Accept the idea that you may have to go on ten dates before finding someone who you want to see a second time. This statistic is supported by some basic and simple research that I have done on this topic. Men and women seem to think this one in ten ratio is "on the mark." If you find Mr. or Ms. Right on your first date, consider yourself to be very lucky.

16. Having said the above, a colleague of mine who happens to be a psychiatrist, met and bonded with a very special man on one of her very first online dates. So, there is hope and miracles do happen.

17. Develop your communication skills. Become a good listener. No one likes an incessant talker. Focus on being interested not interesting.

18. If you have a pleasant date, be sure to let the person know that you enjoyed the time together. A thank you text, phone call or email is a good idea.

19. While many first dates involve meeting for drinks, lunch or dinner, an "activity date" like bowling, hiking, tennis, golf, a walk in the park, or a picnic in a nice spot can be a good way of getting to know each other.

20. If someone is bad about returning your message or messages, do not waste time and energy on them. My experience is that a person who is selfish and unreliable at the start will be unreliable as the relationship moves forward.

21. Some people are on their best behavior when they initially meet you. I suggest that you realize that you may not really know a person until you are in a relationship with them for six or seven months. I mention this six month period several times in this article since I think it is a very useful and important concept. Patients and colleagues have widely supported this idea.

22. Many people who are online are "shopping around." If a relationship develops, the two of you will have to talk about getting off line and focusing on each other exclusively-if your end goal is a long-term relationship. This can be a slippery slope and you may even consider utilizing a therapist to get help with this transition. I talk about this elsewhere in this book.

23. Realize that many people who are online are dating several people simultaneously while they try to identify who is the best match for them. It is likely that you will meet someone who you get on with quite well, but he or she may have some other "irons

in the fire." In some instances, you will be rejected because they may feel that someone else is a better fit. You should not take this personally. You simply can't be right for everyone. If someone has very limited availability, it may mean that they are actively dating one person besides you. Or they might be dating several people. It's part of the online dating world.

24. Another issue that you might encounter is that the person you are dating is wounded due to a recent breakup. They may appear to be blue, depressed and quite needy. Some people will date many people simultaneously because they are sad and empty and they are seeking attention and contact to avoid their loneliness.

25. As I have noted and as you will discover, dating can be emotionally challenging. You may benefit from approaching it as an interpersonal adventure in which you can learn about others and discover a lot about yourself.

26. You will encounter some people who are unreliable or inconsistent in communicating with you. Do not waste time and energy on people who are not being responsive and prompt about returning your messages. I suggest you delete them from your prospect list as soon as possible.

27. Be careful about getting involved with someone who has been married more than three times.

28. Be careful about connecting with someone who is estranged from many or all of their family members.

29. Look for a relationship in which you both function as peers or as CO-CEO's.

30. Avoid someone who has to be right all the time.

31. Avoid someone who is rigid and inflexible.

32. Great sex can be alluring, seductive and fantastic. However, it is only one component of a relationship.

33. Remember, connecting with one very special person can make all your efforts worthwhile.

34. Your imagination, your fantasies and your daydreams play a role in online dating. Now, many worthwhile things start as a dream, a daydream or a fantasy of some kind. Envisioning success can be very useful. I think people who are online and who are looking for a long-term relationship believe or hope that the next person they meet will be the right one. Moreover, this kind of thinking can help them to remain motivated and to continue the search. However, this kind of thinking can also cause a person to feel disappointed if they have a bad run and they experience a few bad dates in a row. As I have said elsewhere in this book, if you find that one very special person, your time and energy is probably well spent. So, remain optimistic and hopeful, but expect some disappointments along the way, as you go through this process. It's a bit like fishing, if you put ten lines in the water, you may only catch one nice fish. Similarly, if you make contact with ten people, perhaps only one will be a good catch or a good match for you.

35. Be patient as you go through the meeting process and try not to get ahead of yourself. Get good at staying in the present and in the here and now as the relationship evolves. Learn to separate your fantasies from what is happening in reality between you and the person or persons you are dating.

36. Look for a person who treats you with kindness, dignity and respect-all the time.

37. Look for an individual who demonstrates kindness to family members, friends, pets, the elderly, waiters and waitresses.

38. Determine if the two of you can problem solve as teammates.

39. Some people have no ability to discuss feelings and solutions to problems. I have dated a few people like this. I strongly suggest that you avoid people who lack these skills.

40. Make sure there is a good deal of laughter and levity when you are together.

41. You may want to avoid people who have been physically abused, emotionally abused or sexually abused. Intimacy, trust and closeness can be troublesome for people who have been damaged in one or more of these aforementioned manners.

42. Be curious about people who have not dated for many years or who have been single for many years. They may be somewhat fixed in their lifestyle and may not be capable of sharing their lives with someone.

43. It takes time to really get to know someone. As my friend who is a psychiatrist told me, "You need to know someone through the four seasons to really know them."

44. If you are thinking of getting married or living with someone you are dating, remember and realize that a stormy courtship will more than likely generate a story marriage. Getting married rarely cures or fixes an unhealthy relationship.

45. I would again remind you that you do not really know someone until you go through a few conflicts with them.

46. While online dating allows you to meet a lot of people, relationships will require work, energy, good communication, kindness, flexibility, trust, humor, and a bunch of other qualities. Some of these elements are mentioned elsewhere in this book.

47. Some people who are dating on the web may be wounded, hurt, disappointed, angry and frustrated because they have experienced disappointment and rejection from meeting a lot of

people but have not been able to discover that special long-term relationship. As I have said elsewhere, this form of meeting people can be challenging.

48. Dating in middle age or older can be much tougher than it is when compared to dating in your thirties. People are more set in their ways and many bring "emotional baggage" from failed relationships, losses and deaths.

49. If you get really close with someone and are uncertain about whether you can make a go of things, consider living together for six to nine months to see how the relationship grows.

50. If you get into a conflict with someone you are dating, do not rely on text and emails to communicate. These forms of communication can often create additional issues due to misunderstandings. To be honest, I, myself, have learned this the hard way and made this mistake. Two of my relationships collapsed, in part, because of misunderstandings caused by electronic communication. Use face to face communication, the phone or video to resolve conflicts and to sort out important issues.

51. Connect with a therapist or dating coach if you think you need some guidance, support and encouragement through this process.

HOW TO REALLY FAIL AT ONLINE DATING

One of my patients recently asked me to list the top reasons that cause people to fail or have little success at online dating. Here are some of the reasons that people do not find the right companion online.

1. Posting photos that are not current can turn people off when you meet them.

2. Posting photos that are unflattering. Hire a photographer and post six attractive and interesting photos.

3. Posting photos that are unclear and have poor lighting.

4. Posting a bio or a profile that is boring, unappealing, unwelcoming and fails to generate a high of number of quality respondents.

5. Lie in your bio or profile. This will come back to haunt you at some point.

6. Being too demanding, controlling and perfectionistic will turn a lot of potential companions off in a hurry.

7. Failing to invest the time and energy needed to be successful at meeting people in this manner. You need to spend about an hour a day to have success.

8. You are doing something to turn people off when you meet them face to face. Most likely, you are dominating the conversation and trying to impress them. That is, you are so concerned with being interesting instead of interested that you are repelling people.

9. You have little self-awareness and poor interpersonal skills and you simply don't know how to build and cultivate a long-term relationship.

10. You are mentally and physically exhausted from spending too much time and energy scanning the sites and the apps.

11. You are not utilizing Zoom, Facetime, or another video platform to meet and screen people. This technology can save time, energy and money and allows you to get a feeling for the person before you meet them. It also helps you to determine if there is

some chemistry between the two of you. I have started to use video technology in my personal life and in my practice and found it to be enormously helpful.

THE GOAL FOR DATE NUMBER ONE

It is quite common for people to get ahead of themselves when they start dating someone they like. Hormones, hopes and fantasies get activated and people start to get way ahead of themselves.

All you need to sort out on date number one is whether or not you want to see the person on date number two.

You also want to determine if there is "good chemistry" between the two of you.

WHO SHOULD PAY FOR THE FIRST DATE?

You have some options as to how you want to handle the finances on the first date.

I almost always pay because I can afford it and I like doing it.

However, whether you are male or female, either one of you can suggest splitting the bill.

You can also offer to pay for the tip.

If the date goes well, you can offer to pay for the next dinner, lunch or round of drinks.

If one of you makes or has a lot more money than the other person, you may want to pay more and pay more often.

Some men like to pay for everything.

Some women like to have the man pay for everything. One woman who I dated who was a physician became quite angry with me about this issue. After taking her out a dozen times and paying for everything, I told her it would be nice if she took me out for breakfast, lunch or dinner once in a while.

She became very angry with me and to make matters worse, she refused to even discuss a possible solution. Now, mind you, I was not asking for very much in return. One dinner a month would have been fine. Understandably, this quasi-relationship ended shortly thereafter.

I am much more comfortable dating a woman who is willing to be a bit less thrifty and a bit more generous.

And, by the way, I have dated many women who are perfectly ok with two adults being kind and generous to one another. In fact, some have insisted on paying for evenings out.

Another lady, who also happened to be a physician said, "If you are sleeping with a woman, the man should definitely pay for everything."

To me, this sounded a lot like prostitution.

Another woman who I dated a few times, never said thank you for the expensive dinners I paid for. This was a huge turnoff to me and I only saw her twice.

As you probably know, money can be a thorny issue.

As your relationship evolves, see if you can get to a comfortable plan regarding finances that is right for both of you.

MORE ON CHEMISTRY AND ONLINE DATING

1. If you read the bios and profiles on the dating sites, you will see that most people are very interested in "chemistry."

For me and I think for most people, I know I need to have that magical kind of attraction to move forward in a romantic relationship.

This magical attraction and the energy that goes with it encourages playfulness, hand holding, hugging, walking arm and arm, flirting, sex and make up sex. These are all valuable and important behaviors.

I think it is a good idea to speak openly as to whether you both feel that there is "chemistry" and a mutual attraction to one another. If the mutual attraction is there, you can spend time getting to know each other better on the first date. If it is not there, I suggest that you both might want to cut your losses, part as friends and move on to the next prospect. This direct conversation will save you time, money and energy.

2. Not every male or female is wired in this manner. However, as I said above, I believe this kind of chemistry can add a lot of joy, romance, and fun to a love relationship.

3. Recently, I dated a new woman who was very successful and very bright. However, she was simply not someone with whom I could imagine being intimate. She wanted to see me again, but a half hour after our first date, I texted her and I said that the chemistry was just not there for me. Like most people, I don't like to hurt anybody, but I thought this was the honest and kind thing to do, given the circumstances.

4. Now, some therapists suggest that you approach dating with an open mind and give yourself a chance to get to know your date.

They suggest having three dates before deciding how you feel about a new person. There is nothing terrible about this advice. I guess the chemistry issue is just quite important to me.

A BIT MORE ON CHEMISTRY.......

On a date I had some time ago, a woman and I spoke about how important chemistry was to us when we sat down for dinner.

We determined and shared that "the chemistry" was there for both of us. The evening was super and we dated for quite a while.

I suggest that some daters benefit from including a discussion about the presence or absence of this essential chemistry early on in the dating process.

If it is not there for both of you, shake hands, wish each other luck and walk away to date another day.

If it is there, it can be a good sign and things can be quite enjoyable and exciting. This does not mean that "you are a match made in heaven." But, it can mean you have an element that can be enjoyable and can get things off to a good start.

I know that some people, including my colleagues who are therapists, will find the above to be crass, shallow and perhaps even unfair. I just don't agree.

Again, if so many internet daters mention chemistry as being important, why not determine whether it is there or not there early on?

By the way, you may be able to determine whether or not there is chemistry by a Zoom conference, Facetime or another audio visual app. These approaches can save you a lot of time, money, and energy. So, give this high tech methodology some thought if the chemistry factor is important to you.

ONE ADDITIONAL AND NEW THOUGHT ON CHEMISTRY, ATTRACTION AND ATTRACTIVENESS

Recently, I dated a woman who I was not that attracted to initially. However, she did become more beautiful as I got to know her. In fact, one night during a sunset dinner, I made a point of telling her that she looked gorgeous.

She really did become more beautiful as I got to know her. I think I was drawn to her intellect, her interesting career and the fact that she was quite complimentary toward me. She was also a great listener and a very devoted mother.

I think this was the first time that I had experienced this phenomenon where someone became more beautiful as the courtship got longer. I found this experience to be enlightening and very interesting.

STRESS MANAGEMENT FOR ONLINE DATERS

Online dating can be rather stressful. Here are a few more tips for maintaining your emotional and physical wellness during your search.

1. Expect to meet some liars.

2. Expect to meet some creeps.

3. You will experience some rejection. So, develop a thick skin.

4. Remain curious about this adventure.

5. Limit yourself to no more than two to three dates per week.

6. Spend time with your passions and hobbies.

7. Spend time with supportive friends and family members.

8. If you have a friend who is dating online, share your experiences, your war stories, your funny dates, your cool dates, your sexual encounters, and your love and support for one another.

9. Spend time with nature: gardening, fishing, hiking, swimming in a lake, or in the ocean.

10. Develop a sense of humor if you don't have one. You will need to develop one. (As some of you know, I won second place in the funniest therapist in New York some years ago. I have recently written an entire comedy routine about online dating. It is a great source of material.)

11. Learn meditation.

12. Learn mindful meditation.

13. Get some training in self-hypnosis

14. Visualize successful dates.

15. Imagine successful relationships.

16. You may find that you discover new friends as well as new lovers on the web.

17. Engage in exercise three to five times a week.

18. Your heart may be broken during the course of your dating and it can take time for this emotional wound to heal. If you struggle for an extended period of time after a break up, you may want to get some therapy or counseling.

19. Dating later in life is more complicated than it was in your earlier years. People can be set in their ways. People have extended

families which can complicate relationships. People may be wounded because of a bitter divorce. Or, they can be sad because of the death of a spouse. Dating can create some anxiety for people who are shy by nature. As noted earlier, people may be dating several people simultaneously and they may be less than honest, genuine and open at times. Develop a thick skin to get your mind and your body ready for these challenges.

20. Learn a new hobby, sport, skill or activity.

21. Try to get the same amount of sleep every night.

22. Drink at least eight glasses of water a day.

23. Start every day with a recognition of what you are grateful for and thankful for.

24. If you are spiritual or religious, utilize prayer and your faith to keep your spirits up.

25. Listen to your favorite music and dance if you feel like it.

26. Sing in the shower even if you have a terrible voice.

27. Online dating can be challenging and stressful. But, many people feel it is a lot better than trying to meet Mr. Right or Ms. Right by hanging out at a bar.

28. Online dating is a little like being at a buffet. If you find someone you like, spend more time with him or her. If you meet someone who is not to your liking and not right for you, best to spend less time with that person and to "cut your losses" and walk away. Save your time and energy for the people who seem to be really special.

29. You may want to view online dating as a kind of hobby. I recently suggested this to a patient of mine and she thought this was a good idea and she felt that approaching it as "a hobby"

would help her to avoid dating too much and find a way to enjoy the dating process.

30. Realize that you will go on first dates where you think everything is terrific and your partner expresses their joy about the evening. Then a few hours later or a few days later, you learn that they want to end the connection. Understand that people are frequently dating several people at the same time they are seeing you. In addition, some people are disingenuous and they like to lead another person on. Furthermore, people can be fickle and say things that they mean in the moment, but are not really true. As I have said elsewhere in this book, you need to have a thick skin in the electronic dating world. Be patient, pace yourself and don't take the rejection or shift in attitude personally. You cannot please everyone you meet and there are instances where you may decide that someone is not quite right for you.

31. Spend some of your time helping others. Consider volunteering, community service or raising money for a good cause.

32. Don't put all your "emotional eggs" into online dating. Make sure you have other sources of joy in your life. This kind of balance is essential.

33. Learn the serenity prayer and practice it often.
    https://en.wikipedia.org/wiki/Serenity_Prayer

SHOULD YOU DATE MORE THAN ONE PERSON AT A TIME?

The answer is yes. The idea of having "a few lines in the water" or "a few irons in the fire" seems to make sense to me. I think that dating three people at one time is probably the maximum amount that makes any sense.

When you meet someone who is really special, you can let go of the other people to focus on this "special pal."

Having said the above, some people like to date just one person at a time and that is certainly their prerogative and it is perfectly ok.

A BIT MORE ABOUT THE DATING SITES

Online dating can be exhausting and a person can get burnt out after partaking in this process for an extended period of time. Searching through profiles and photos, reaching out to others and responding to inquiries can be extremely time consuming. So, taking a break is often a wise idea.

Some people have a very hard time getting off the dating apps. In some cases, people want to keep dating as a kind of "insurance policy" in case their current relationship or relationships do not work out. This can be thought of as a self-protective act designed to avoid the emotional pain and loss which accompany a break up. If you find someone really special, it makes sense to get off line. This can allow you to focus on just one person to determine how you really feel about them and about your relationship.

Remember, you can always get back online if you want to.

Some individuals get "really hooked on" the dating sites and they continue to search for "someone better." They have described it to me as it "being like a kid in a candy store." One woman described her preoccupation with the dating apps as being like "crack cocaine."

Another patient of mine called it dating on steroids.

For some people, setting time limits for viewing the apps and limiting the number of dates you have each week or each month can be quite helpful.

Also, taking a complete break or trying a different app can help you avoid burnout and expose you to a new critical mass of potential mates. If you experiment a bit, you will probably discover the app that is right for your needs, wants and goals.

Getting off the sites can sometimes become a sticky and complicated issue for a couple. This can be a significant source of friction if one member of the relationship wants to get off the site(s) and the other member wants to remain on the site(s).

I would suggest that you and your partner discuss this issue openly and honestly and try to discover a time frame and a plan that works for both of you.

Obviously, if you fall in love and develop a relationship that is healthy, loving, growing and thriving, it is probably time to concentrate your energy and attention on this one special person. Some people can become quite addicted to the dating sites. Realize that if you genuinely want a long-term, monogamous relationship, you probably have to focus on just one person at a certain point in time.

Some of the sites will allow you to suspend your membership and then to return at a later date.

Again, as I said earlier, if things don't work out, it is pretty easy to get back in the game.

ANOTHER SENSIBLE WAY TO GET OFF THE DATING SITE OR DATING SITES

If you and your partner feel that you are developing strong feelings for one another, you may want to agree to get off the site and date each other exclusively and revisit this issue in ninety days.

GETTING OFF THE SITES "NATURALLY"

Some couples develop similar feelings for one another at the same time. In one relationship that I had, we never needed to discuss this. Apparently, we were drawn to one another and we completely trusted each other. We both simply agreed it was time to focus on one another exclusively.

MANAGING BREAK UPS

Expect to have a few break ups as you search for that special person. These "endings" can be emotional and painful. As I have told many of my patients over the years, a break up is a lot like a wound or an injury that needs time and tender loving care to heal.

During the past thirty-three months, I've been through six or seven breakups. I initiated some of these. Some were initiated by the other side.

I try to learn what I can from these experiences and I make an effort to not make the same mistakes over and over again.

As I say elsewhere in this book, it takes time to really get to know a person and determine if the two of you can create a healthy relationship.

The end of a relationship can trigger sadness, anxiety and depression.

Reach out and utilize your friends, family and support network as you ride out this emotional storm.

If you want to "get back in the game" and are emotionally ready to start dating, the internet makes it very easy to do this. And for some people this can be an effective way to help heal the wound that you might feel after the collapse of a relationship.

If sad feelings and a prolonged depression of symptoms persist, you may want to contact a mental health professional.

WHAT YOU NEED TO HAVE A VIBRANT, HEALTHY, LOVING AND FUN RELATIONSHIP

In my psychotherapy practice, I am currently counseling a number of people who are using online dating in order to discover that special person. It has caused me to think about the qualities that help to build an enduring connection.

What follows is a list of positive characteristics which will increase the likelihood of developing a healthy connection.

The next section in this piece will delineate some more of the things you want to have in your relationship.

Much of the information in these sections is based on my experiences with couples and single people during the last thirty-five years as well as my own dating experiences.

In addition, some of the information is based on my thirty-two years of experience in an absolutely outstanding marriage.

1.   As I noted elsewhere, find a mate who you feel really lucky to have in your life.

2. Connect with someone who you find physically attractive.

3. Select a mate who has an abundance of healthy relationships with friends and family members.

4. Choose a partner who is flexible and who does not always have to be right.

5. Find someone who does some altruistic work in his or her life.

6. Pick a person who does not take himself or herself too seriously.

7. Find someone with whom you can laugh a lot.

8. Select a mate who can share tasks with you.

9. Pick a person who is good at what you are bad at.

10. Do not look for a perfect person.

11. Team up with a person who has good problem solving skills and good communication skills.

12. Find someone who fits in well with your friends and family members.

13. It is great if you share some interests with another person. And it is also nice if you can teach each other some new things.

14. It is also terrific if you have separate hobbies and interests.

15. Since a lot of couples break up over money issues, choose someone with whom you can manage finances in an effective and intelligent manner.

16. Get good at compromising. Focus on being happy, not on being right.

17. Look for someone who shares some of the same dreams and goals that you have.

18. Make sure your partner treats you with kindness, dignity, and respect all the time.

19. Discover a mate who loves you no matter what.

20. A person who is a loving and devoted parent can be a predictor of someone who can be a good spouse.

21. A spouse who is willing to apologize and say that he or she is sorry can be a great companion.

22. Find someone who you can look forward to growing older with.

23. Pick a person who adds to the peace and tranquility in your life.

24. Connect with a mate who makes life easier.

25. Remember, opposites can attract.

26. Pick someone who is an intellectual peer.

27. Be with someone from whom you can learn.

28. You can really enjoy someone who encourages you and picks you up when you are down.

29. Spend time studying and modeling couples with healthy relationships.

30. Pick a pal who can help you get through life's ups and downs.

31. Find a mate with whom you can enjoy doing nothing.

32. A healthy, adventurous and active sex life is a big plus. So, connect with someone with whom you can enjoy an intimate life.

33. Listening is a very important part of communicating.

34. It is a benefit and a bonus if your lover can get along well with in-laws and extended family members. Having said this, I would remind you that couples frequently have to make each other a priority ahead of in-laws and extended family members. As I have told many couples, "When you walk down the aisle, you say "I do" to each other, not to your in-laws.

35. Be certain that you and your significant other share dreams and goals.

36. Gravitate towards someone who demonstrates kindness to pets, animals, elders, kids and strangers.

37. As I have said many times, "People can be very complicated and relationships can be even more complicated."

38. In the early stages of a relationship, things should be easy and simple.

39. Pay close attention to how well the two of you problem solve together.

40. Look for a companion who will make your life easier.

41. Having a partner who is open to getting some coaching or counseling when needed can make it easier to problem solve effectively as a team.

42. My wife and I used to say that we were a great team. I think that was true. In fact, we described ourselves as a "dream team" in our wedding vows.

CHALLENGES, OPPORTUNITIES AND ADVENTURES

As a relationship develops, there will be a number of challenges, opportunities and adventures. Here are a few of them.

1. When and how should you become intimate with one another?

2. What can you do to get physically comfortable with one another?

3. As I noted earlier, when and how should you get off the dating sites?

4. Meeting a person's family and friends can be a bit overwhelming. However, it can be an opportunity to have some additional loving people in your life.

5. Traveling can teach you a lot about each other and help you to get to know each other better. Consider going on a trip or vacation after you have been dating for a few months. Planning a trip and traveling can demonstrate if there is good teamwork between the two of you. When you travel, you frequently have to deal with schedule changes, bad weather and airport delays. Be mindful of how the two of you navigate these obstacles.

WHAT YOU DON'T NEED IN YOUR RELATIONSHIP

Now, I will move into a discussion of some of the characteristics, patterns, behaviors and attitudes that can create problems for couples.

1. Avoid someone who is physically abusive or who has a history of being physically abusive.

2. Similarly, avoid someone who is emotionally abusive.

3. Stay away from a person who has had a history of being in unstable and unhealthy relationships.

4. Never connect with a drug addict or alcoholic.

5. Avoid dating a workaholic. I dated a high achieving, Type A personality who was the CEO of an organization. It was clear after a few months that she simply had no time and energy for us or for a healthy relationship.

6. Similarly, a compulsive gambler is usually not a good long-term companion.

7. Compulsive shoppers can be difficult to stay connected to.

8. Trust is very important in a relationship. Consequently, being involved with a chronic liar is a prescription for disaster.

9. A person who has been married more than three times may be difficult to build a relationship with.

10. A person with no friends can be problematic.

11. A rigid person who has to have his or her way and has to be right all the time is tough to stay connected to.

12. Someone who wants to move in and/or get married very quickly may be problematic.

13. An unstable job history can be a cause for concern.

14. Avoid a person with a criminal past or criminal background.

15. A person with a history of infidelity may be tough to trust.

16. Like other addictions, a sexual addiction can be a deal breaker for a healthy relationship.

17. A person who had unloving parents and an unstable home life may struggle in a monogamous relationship.

18. A person with a serious, untreated, mental illness can be very hard to share your life with.

19. You don't need a person with a history of financial instability.

20. You don't need a person with an unstable work history.

21. If your courtship is stormy and dysfunctional, your marriage is likely to be similar or worse.

22. Avoid someone who has difficulty managing anger.

23. Everyone likes to be treated nicely. However, one woman was showering me with expensive gifts early in our relationship. Initially, I thought this was very nice. However, when it continued for a while, I realized she was trying to "buy my attention and affection," and there was a hidden agenda behind her

generosity. She also seemed to want my undivided attention all the time. I ended this relationship about three weeks after it began. So, sometimes we need to examine someone who is overly nice and wanting a lot of our attention from "the get go."

24. Stay away from someone who has difficulty sharing his or her feelings in an open and honest manner. Some of the women I dated seemed quite mature and stable until they became frustrated or hurt or angry. When faced with these feelings some of them would shut down, withdraw and demonstrate little capacity to communicate and problem solve. One of them would have what I would call an adult temper tantrum over small disappointments. Not surprisingly, this relationship lasted just several months.

25. Marriage counseling, psychotherapy and counseling can help remedy some of the issues on this list.

26. If you have doubts or concerns, pre-marital counseling with a licensed mental health professional can be a good idea and a wise investment. In all likelihood, your relationship will fall into one of these three categories:

You are a great team and seem like you are terrific for one another.

There are some significant issues and you should either part or seek couples therapy.

Your relationship is okay, but one or both of you has some reservations about the viability of your relationship. In this case, you may find it useful to live together for six to nine months and see how you feel about one another. Again, therapy may also be useful during this trial period.

EVERYTHING WORTHWHILE BEGINS WITH A DREAM OR A DAYDREAM

If you are reading this blog, you probably have a fantasy, a hope, a dream or a daydream of meeting and connecting with that very special person.

These daydreams and night dreams can be powerful motivators and they can play a powerful role in facilitating self-awareness and in promoting change and growth.

Recognizing this, some years ago, I developed a therapeutic approach that I called Cognitive Behavioral Dream Therapy.

Here is how this model works:

First, identify the kind of person and the kind of relationship you are wanting to connect without being too perfectionistic. This is your "dream."

Second, ask yourself what attitudes, thoughts and behaviors and feelings you need to change, modify or put energy into in order to increase the likelihood of meeting and connecting with this kind of individual.

For example, you may realize that you need to lose some weight, post better photos, rewrite your bio or profile, remain optimistic, be open to introductions as well as online dating, move to a place which is densely populated and do a better job of listening during your first date.

These kinds of behavioral and cognitive shifts can increase the likelihood that your dream will become a reality.

Some of you will elect to change your thoughts first and then change your behavior.

Others will make behavioral changes first.

And some of you may change a feeling or a group of feelings first.

How you implement this model depends on how you are wired and how you go about completing tasks, accomplishing goals and converting your dreams to realities.

You may also find that this model can help with making changes in other parts of your life.

Many of my patients have used this approach to make important changes in their life including: changing careers, starting a business, getting a promotion, quitting smoking, losing weight and moving to a new city or country.

So, pay very close attention to your dream and modify your thoughts, feelings and behaviors to make your dreams a reality.

If you would like to talk to me about learning and utilizing this method, you can reach me at info@stayinthezone.com or at 201 647-9191.

PERSONAL EXPERIENCES VS. CLINICAL EXPERIENCES

In a previous version of this book, I had included a long section on my dating experiences. As I think I noted earlier, I have dated ninety-one different women since my wife's passing almost three years ago.

Most of these dates were "one and done." I did, however, have a half a dozen relationships that lasted from three months to seven months.

Some of these dating experiences were humorous. (In fact, as some of you know, I have done some stand-up comedy in the past. And I do have an entire comedy routine about online dating.) I believe that a sense of humor is a valuable coping tool for managing stress or for handling any of life's challenges.

Some of the other dates were disappointing, frustrating, confusing or sad. Only a handful of the people were really unpleasant. Most of the time, I viewed these dates as learning experiences and as adventures in interpersonal relationships.

While I thought that sharing these experiences could be quite useful, I have decided to not include these personal experiences as I do not want to offend, embarrass or hurt any of the people I dated.

In lieu of including my personal dating experiences, I have decided to include in the current version of this book a collection of cases involving single people who learned how to better navigate the dating process with the utilization of sport psychology tools and techniques and hypnosis. This section appears in the pages that follow.

SPORT PSYCHOLOGY AND MENTAL TOUGHNESS TRAINING FOR ONLINE DATERS

As I noted in a previous article that I wrote, many of the sport psychology techniques I have taught to elite athletes, weekend warriors, young athletes, executives, stock traders, performing artists and CEO's can be quite useful for online daters.

I thought it would be helpful and interesting to share some case histories showing how I used sport psychology techniques to help people who are searching for love on the internet.

I think the readers of this book will find these anecdotes to be quite interesting and instructive.

Having goals, objectives, daydreams and dreams are useful in sports and in relationships.

Similarly, knowing how to be relaxed, confident, focused, optimistic, curious, adventurous, peaceful, playful, open, flexible, resilient, resourceful and hard-working are all qualities that everyone can benefit from using in sports and in life and in relationships. My main website is called StayInTheZone.com

In short, as my website's name implies, I teach people how to get into the zone and stay there.

Because the hypnotic state of mind parallels the zone, hypnosis and self-hypnosis often play a powerful role in activating the aforementioned qualities. I teach these skills to athletes and to couples who are wanting to perform better in their sports, in their careers and in their relationships.

Sometimes, I hypnotize both members of a marriage or a couple to help them discover new and better ways of managing stress, problem solving, eliminating destructive behaviors and replacing them with positive ways of being and interacting.

Hypnosis can activate a person's unconscious mind and help them to discover creative solutions to problems which their conscious mind could not access.

Interestingly, some self-hypnotic techniques can help couples to argue less, communicate more effectively, lower stress and end or reduce marital or relationship discord.

I have developed a number of books, videos and audio programs about hypnosis and about getting into the zone. https://stayinthezone.com/shop/

You can learn more about these techniques by visiting www.StayInTheZone.com.

And if you need a therapist, coach, and experienced writer to help you manage and improve your search for that very special, wonderful, life changing person, you can email me at info@stayinthezone.com or you can call me at 888 580-ZONE.

SPORT PSYCHOLOGY AND ONLINE DATING CASE HISTORIES

Case History # 1:
Visualization

Top athletes use visualization to crystalize and achieve their goals.

I have suggested that daters spend some time creating in their minds exactly the kind of relationship they are seeking.

I encourage them to be very specific and to place the relationship in exactly the kind of environment that they love to be in.

I encourage them to imagine that they create and experience a vibrant relationship that lasts for many years.

Try doing this simple visualization exercise twice a day for about twenty minutes at a time.

Note what you observe, learn, discover and what you enjoy.

And be aware of how your body feels as you do this exercise.

I recall doing this exercise with one man and he discovered that he needed someone who was retired like he was as he wanted to be able to spend a lot of time with his mate. Someone who was still working would not have been available enough for this fellow.

Sport Psychology Case History #2:
Risk Taking

Several years ago, a psychologist came to see me to become more comfortable with taking risks in the online dating world.

She had been divorced twice before and she was afraid of making a wrong choice again.

I hypnotized her and told her one story about how people get into the ocean on a sunny day. Some run in and dive into the waves or dive above the waves as fast and as high as they can.

Others walk in slowly and sprinkle water on their wrists, shoulders and backs to get used to the temperature of the water.

But eventually all the swimmers and beachgoers get into the water, enjoy the escape from the heat and get to experience the wonderful feeling of refreshing salt water on a hot day.

Obviously, this metaphor was intended to help her move ahead in her dating life at a pace at which she was comfortable.

After this hypnotic session, she began taking social risks both online and offline.

Sport Psychology Case History #3:
Perseverance And Mental Toughness

The process of online dating can be very frustrating and challenging. In addition, as I noted earlier, you can expect some emotional challenges along the way.

To activate a person's perseverance and mental toughness, I suggest that they try taking an ice cold shower for as long as they can stand the temperature and that they expand the time they stay in the shower by five seconds every day for two weeks.

This simple exercise seems to build both mental toughness and perseverance.

Sport Psychology Case #4:
Building Confidence For The First Date

Some people get very anxious prior to a first date. Some even get anxious prior to their first phone call with a new person.

Role playing is a great way to get mentally ready for your first date. Practice, listening, paraphrasing what your date might say, asking questions and breathing deeply to relax your mind and your body.

Imagine that you handle all the challenges that you can experience on a date with grace, ease and confidence.

Sport Psychology Case#5:
Discovering Your Inner Champion

Like sports, dating online successfully requires courage, resourcefulness, creativity, resilience, patience, stamina, practice, a thick skin and an open mind.

Ask yourself, what was the toughest challenge you had to face in your life? Once you identify what helped you to succeed at this challenge, you may want to apply these same skills to behaviors and attitudes to your online dating adventures.

WHAT ARE THE TEN MOST IMPORTANT TIPS IN THIS BOOK?

Recently, a client of mine asked me what I thought were the ten most important takeaways from this book.

Here are my best thoughts on this matter.

1. Take one date at a time.

2. Remember, it takes six months to really get to know a person.

3. Expect to have one good date for every ten people that you meet.

4. Don't forget that you are in a search for just one special lover.

5. Practice The Serenity Prayer two times a day.

6. Develop and use a network of friends and relatives who can support you as you go through the dating process.

7. Have a good idea of what kind of person you are looking for.

8. Be certain that your bio, profile and photos are as appealing as possible.

9. Know when you need to work harder at your search and know when you need to take a break.

10. Seek out the services of a coach or a therapist who can help you through the ups and downs of this process.

ABOUT THE AUTHOR

Jay P. Granat, Ph.D., is a Psychotherapist, Hypnotherapist and Licensed Marriage and Family Counselor.

Dr. Granat has counseled thousands of individuals, couples and families during the last thirty years.

He has coached many people through the divorce, separation, healing, dating and mating process. After the passing of his wife, he, himself, utilized online dating to discover a companion who was right for him.

A former university professor, Dr. Granat has written a weekly column for five newspapers and has appeared in many major media outlets including: The New York Times, The Wall Street Journal, Good Morning America, USA Today, Sports Illustrated, The International Herald Tribune, The BBC, The New York State Bar Journal, Legal Economics, USA Today, The Bergen Record, The New York Post, The Rehabilitation Counseling Bulletin, New York Magazine, ESPN, Golf Digest, Success Magazine, and others.

Granat earned his Master's degree and Ph.D. in Counseling from The University of Michigan. His undergraduate work was completed at The State University Of New York At Buffalo. He has written six books and developed a dozen self-help audio programs and video programs.

Dr. Granat has coached many people through the divorce process and guided them through the dating and meeting processes. His dissertation focused on marriage, relationships and divorce.

He is past Vice President of The New York Society For Ericksonian Psychotherapy and Hypnosis.

Dr. Granat has an interest in comedy and won third place in the funniest therapist in New York contest. He encourages people to use humor as one important strategy for managing many kinds of stress.

This book is dedicated to my late wife.

Robin taught me, my kids and anyone who ever met her an abundance about teamwork, about love and about relationships.